UMBRA

for Jamie
with a poet's
soul and a
wonderful zest
for life.
Love,
Myrna

10·2·04

UMBRA

Poems by

Myrna Patterson

To order additional copies of this book, contact:
Xlibris Corporation
1-888-795-4274
www.Xlibris.com
Orders@Xlibris.com
21449

CONTENTS

I

II

for Daniel

Yesterday was glory and joy.
Today, a blackened burn everywhere.

On the record of my life, these two days
will be put down as *one*.

Rumi

What is to give light
must endure burning.

Victor Frankl

I

River Hymn

Not gull whine and squawk
over a small hum of cars, not
the oars dipping into the river, not the flag
unfurling high above the distant buildings

but this presentness of citysound
with only a hint of voices
behind massed clumps of trees,
rising from the sweeps on the river.

The silences in-between. Like the breeze
humming around my arms or the sun
vibrating across my face.

    I sit in dark. I sit in light.
        Mind like air. Mind like wind.

Now clouds blanch, disperse, wind slides
down the river, wafts to me, ungraspable.

What moves? What remains?

Barriers

frame the place in the woods where the garden
lay raised on its blue boat in a buttery sea.

Cosmos heap on each other, a rainbow grave
floats, totters under a tree tarp.

Who put you here, carved
a trough in a tight pine stand,

layered the ground with yellow cloak
spread like an empty picnic blanket?

Who closed you in? Blue post
spikes pierce the citron gloss

reflect black trunks beyond
but cut down, chipped teeth.

Havoc! The sea tilts and buckles.

Quagmire

Home was a bottomland, a dark
turmoil of bodies wedged, suffocating.

When she cursed and screamed,
floor became quicksand. No

hiding place here. Learn
to push through, to float.

Aubade

"il n'est mie jors . . . ."
Provençal, 12th or 13th century

It is not yet daylight, not yet that rosyfingered
promise of shelter from murky phantoms
who slither in my bed all night.

I hold tight to my pillow on the turbulent sea.
Close my ears to the dull thud and grind
of giant beasts stalking in the murk.

Whirling in bleak space, alone, trembling,
I am a grey heron, perched above the waters
of chaos, breaking the silence with a cry,

asking what is, what is not to be.
Waves of yellow light slide out of blackness,
ignite dawn's roseate glow. I awake.

Kavanah

Late afternoon
 the hawk
  rises up
   over the field

over the lolling groups
 of students
  seeking
   precise words

over the mute fear
 of those who
  would be seen
   exposed

and I say: look!
 taut wings lift
  the hawk through
   fierce winds

his solo-stunt
 erasing us
  as if only flight
   matters.

Drift

Even
even if
even uneven
evening.

It is evening and
not yet night,
not yet the cold
hour of grief.

The last ones fall
and vanish.
The ones
who held me
                    naked
on the earth.

Untethered, I float.
    I dance.

Flight

I couldn't run fast enough.
Roller skates, bicycles.
Climbing trees, hanging upside down.

Two sisters were in charge of corralling me,
the untamable, the wild girl,
vilda heya, Grandmother chanted.

What could I have done when I was so bad
but try to be better than good?

What to do now in the twilight, left like
Gretel, but push her into the flaming oven?

Abyss

She tried, she really did,
not to land on them,
leapt over them,
rolled and twirled
then circled back.
The cracks drew her
Still. Still. Below, where
the dank, dark cellar
of her life waited,
as if she could crawl into
the narrow lines, disappear
where her mother could
not come.

Because of a girl
Mother's back would break.

Morning Glory

On those cold summer mornings, I awoke
to the sound of keys jingling,
to my father, eager to leave.

For a few hours, I was the chosen.
Ten years old, and I could sit next
to him on an aqua stool,

eating buttery, syrup-soaked, French toast.
At the harbor we rented a rowboat.
I carried the box of wriggling worms,

sat tall in the middle seat, waiting for him
to set the oars in their locks. I rowed
and rowed across the harbor, hands blistering,

never once winced at the sight of worms,
caught a flounder, gave it up,
willingly, to him.

Anatta

The firmament presses
its grey hand upon me.

Clouds cross a silent sky.

I am here, burrowing
in my old skin and bones,
breathing them.

I am no thing, no
sound no where.

Dialogue

Sandbars stretch before me, brown backs speckled.
Gulls alight, fearless in December's chill
as if all existence rests here on this stretch of shore.

And I, wary of the perfect view, a beach with
shells encrusted, turn my wandering eyes,
seek a cloud that will reveal the light.

Surely I might wade into blue surf,
leave prints in places I have never
trod, and watch them wash away.

Once in airless rooms, I feared the loss of breath,
sought my twin, the happy fearless one
who could break free, be all things.

Yet one sees how those who strayed were lured
by home, a shawl unwound for years,
and planted deep, a waiting golden lamp.

I will not die again, the way
my mother buried me
in brother's grave, denied that I still lived.

The words I write
repair a brittle past.

Ritual

Mother's in the corner again, wedged between
stove and sink, in tattered housedress and
sensible black laced shoes, her head bowed.

She pours the yellow liquid into the hot
buttered pan, tips it to cover the surface,
flips the bubbled circle onto a clean dishcloth
butters, pours, flips. Over and over.

A bowl of filling—cheese, egg, salt—
awaits. She plops a spoonful in the middle
of a cooled crepe, begins the slow folding
and crimping. The edge of her tongue
over her lip in perfect concentration.

An army of small yellow packets in rows await
the sauté pan. She continues, never turns
to see her youngest daughter behind her.

Syncopation

The same breakfast:
    toast, sanka
The same lunch:
    cottage cheese
    hard boiled egg
The same tasks. In the same order.
week after week. year after year:
Wash on Monday; Iron on Tuesday.
Shop on Thursday (serve fish).
Hairdresser on Friday (chicken).

            *

Now a helpless child at 94—
    numb, gnarled hands
    buckling legs
    dim eyes.

Tiny, in the hospital bed,
she awaits
    the tray of food
    the bed pan

Her daughter
Brushes her teeth
Smoothes lotion over her parched skin
Teaches her to push the nurse's button
        Feeds her.

Mother says *Thank you*
    for the first time.

Bardo

What will it become? This splitting of
        persons into shadow, leaving
traces   gaps where sunlight hangs
        angular?

Is it that frame-after-frame
                turning
  into a living past? I can do this.

But wait. Is the ceasing what will shape
        this ragged thinness?
  I'm listening for the song of distance and
        delay—to arrange
  us like crumpled curtains.

Flesh and bone remain—helpless,
        bewildered. They'll
  crumble and fade. No matter.

Yes! Matter. Matter. Or is it only the wish-
        fulfilling jewel that will smash through?
  One thousand eyes to see pain
                everywhere,
infiltrate the dark magnet inviting
        every obstacle, every anguish.

Their suffering penetrates,
        wears down the solid
  rock of self I've clung to.
            I see.

Bobie's hands

Gnarled like old trees
from years of washing floors

bulged and twisted
around bands of diamond glitter,

kneading and punching
loaves of heavy black bread,

taming curls to braids
clutching cash

as if it could
set her free.

II

Devotion

What can I say of steadfastness?
How long must I wait to see the heron start
his strut, lift his yellow legs like fishing lines,
place them quick in slippery river mud?

All morning he stands at river's edge, napping
in sullen reeds. Drifting, I dip my paddle
down to knotted lily roots, bring up slimy weeds.
Staring as I float, I see the poem,
its words like silt churned from below.

Now, yellow eye intent, he plunges down
his steely beak, emerges with a fish. That simple.

And why wouldn't he get exactly what he wanted?

Ichthys

for Sara

Sometimes a fish will rest in a hover,
the tides creating a place of light,
peace in the movement of brisk water.
Here in the shallows, a morning fish
lies so, suspended, yet we see
it lives here in this place it loves.

We need to choose love,
to rise from shore, hover
over trees and houses, until we see
the world spread out, clean with light,
the sky reflected, fissionless,
floating, a lily on water.

What does it mean to lie in water,
silent, to love
not moving? If a fish
can survive its element by hovering,
does being still allow the light
to heal rifts in the sea?

We say the real is what we see,
that heavy bodies sink in water,
that only hope exists in light
that, surpassing understanding, love
allows us to forgive, to hover
over muddy streams, green and thick with fish.

By being simple, present, we are fish,
spindles whirling out what we see
below the surface as we hover.
Never sure, in motion, do we water
our hearts with love,
find true nature with the light?

Between earth and heaven, in the light
of day, we create a fissure
in the story of love
then fall into the sea
where fear drowns in transparent water—
all we know, lazing in the hover.

Hovering in morning light, a fish hawk
plunges feet first, in deep love
with water. See him rise, a fish in his talons!

Autumn

Vamp maple, color of ripe lemons, your drama
dwarfs limp blooms beneath. Days darken,
the wheel turns, roses slump haphazardly.

Can I have what is before me,
dark and depleted, harboring spring?
Can I keep them safe?

I could not impede day's end nor keep my children
here with me, could never still the wind
rushing to my dreams, black crows penetrating sleep.

Erev Rosh Hashanah

Some wrongs we can never fully right, I think,
returning to woods heavy with red berries, leaves
yellow streaked, tired branches awaiting sleep.

On this autumn threshold, winds roar up,
swell through brown marsh grasses, churn virgin
waters to grey rippled desert, flinging birds
like kites into the last shards of sun.

Memory rests like dregs at the bottom of a pond.
Rusted cattails genuflect at the edge of whitecaps.

Squalls scream again the second day. A ram's
horn bleats. The missing wait in hollows
nearby. Light hides behind massed clouds.

Gulls fly inland. Two swans protect
their cygnets in the gale.
Breathe. Pray. Let go.

My Dead Brother

After years of holding him,
solid against my child skin
  ceasing to breathe for fear
of unearthing him, I am here
          at last, free
in the thin luminance of autumn dusk
  a fragrance of dried cattails
parched golden.

How could I have known that
he would shimmer
  his translucent light
across the ivory of swans
  and never leave?

Aurora

Snow fell last night
lit trees like candles
in the black vault of sky.

He has left and I am
pregnant with
the memory of him
crashing to the ground
splintered and mute.

In the white night
his soft music
drifts down
blankets the ground.

After the fires of loss,
dawn.

Amaryllis

Ashes do not come back to firewood.
                    Dogen

No one sees it happen.
First, edges wrinkle, turn veiny
a wither from within.
Brazen,
  a pistel flaunts its yellow
            under
a white inviting stigma.

It expects to stay
  and shine,
                  endlessly renewed.
  Instead,
draining to blood red
          it caves
              in
    parched and blind.

Limp beauty closed around its arid sex
  it hangs—weightless
    gasps for breath
                ensnares me
more alive
    for having left.

Stigmata

I watched for days, knowing that a bud
        my smallest finger size
                in tight pink womb
    would unfurl.

A magical slow birth—five veined petals
  from a ruby throat emerged
        beneath
    a stigma yellow-spiked,
filling the air
              with gossamer shimmer.

At dawn the second day, it stood erect.
  Yet, at noon, I found a gnarled hand, fingers clutched
        into each other
             closed
    but for the starburst—
              five red explosions.

Today I cradle a shriveled bud,
      remember you, how you fell
    your face a stripe of blue across the pain.

When they laid your body out, I saw
  the gash upon your cheek,
     spoke
into the limpid air
        It's like you're resting.

So everything changes—
    drowns in raven waters
        while form's
      condensed radiance,
       moves
  back and forth, back and forth.

March Light

There's just no accounting for happiness
the way the winter sky rolls itself up
into a fist of yellow, unfurls
streaming into windows,
across matted brown lawns,
floating in circles
on choppy waves.

I sit on a wooden bench
facing the sea on the anniversary
of his death, watch March light
filter across ragged cattails and
chopped stalks, silent sentinels
to the constant flutter of wings,
crow caws, dogs bounding free
along a narrow trail.

All that exists in the world
is here in this moment
shimmering with new life,
buds pushing out
past last snow traces,
knowing the sun will set,
and rise
and set again.

Sheriff's Meadow
Martha's Vineyard

Brushfoot

At times it rests like an old turtle in the mud,
ignoring its wings, diluting passion into watery gruel.
Or, seduced by the promise of sweet ambrosia, it
quits its swamp, senses rearranged, takes to the air,
antennae tuned to swirls of color, honeyed scents.

After all, there are no guides to show the way. Fearless,
crossing seas, it learns to hitchhike, stays out in the cold.
Dying goes on. Fields empty. It returns to that damp
fire of hope, a mourning cloak, duping the enemy.

Tenacity

Nine tulips remain of the thirty he planted,
loosely scattered among sedum, lilies, vinca.
He simply left, never called again, abandoned
his watch, his rug, his books, his bike.
The lie we lived for years, the breathless gap
into which we poured old tales, wore thin.

Walking through the meadow I hear it.
I know what to do, field glasses raised, waiting,
like he did. A few steps, listen. He'd wait forever
for a bird, stand at the edge of the pond, peering in
or wade into the bulrushes until a fish swam by.

Now the warbler flashes yellow, sings.

Dance

Crouched and touching earth, she reaches
for branches veined and lacy, wears them

like wings, chants for all who cannot sing.
What can she see from behind her mask?

Weak-limbed, we immerse ourselves in a cold stream.
Pulsating light—movement gone mad.

How to illuminate from within that which is dead?
That struggle, that wrestling. Stand up!

Animals begin to wake and sing. A path opens.
Sounds blend and swirl the stagnant air. From a dark

tunnel, we emerge—trees and their
hidden inner hearts, indestructible as bone.

Prayer

Have you fallen into the dark river bottom
where you crouch in a weed tangle,
emerging as glints and glimmers?

Have you hidden suspended in thick storm clouds
filled with static and waiting to be rent,
until you hurled radiant bolts across the sky?

Have you waited beneath the sodden earth,
shuddered under frozen roots and bulbs,
praying for a slow crack through the soil?

Do you live in the wild darkness of my soul,
churn with eddies of fire and throb?
Will you appear, a white song at twilight?

Spring River

No deer drinks from
this muddy swirl, no
wrens chant vespers
as frozen plates of ice
smash in gushing water.

Is this sanctification,
that we must work,
deplete our definition?

A thrilling knell
to what is frozen,
the cadence of a ticking
clock's shrill crack
shivers through us.

Home by Another Way

Today the sea drums, whips itself to froth, the wind
its lover. I am buffeted awake, feel grief,
know that the past lives, that I didn't dream.
Whoever I am can't be apparent.
I become part of all that roars. Dim light
pools inside me, spreads to flames. I seek peace.

My thoughts float as I watch pieces
of seaweed, shell shards, flotsam flung by wind
swept up like feathers, as if they could alight,
agile birds on wisps of wire. My grief,
old as time asks how to be a parent
carry two souls past ruin to a dream

that they choose, let them dream
beyond heavy air, to find a piece
of self, so true and apparent
as to have come from a slight wind.
After all, they feel sunshine, grief
stalks them like a raven its prey, yet lightning

also cracks them open, fills them with light.
I push against chill gusts, sow fragments of a dream
like seeds into hollow furrows, inhale grief
as music against the surf. Sudden peace
arises from my body. The wind
begins a dance, waves roll, their apparent

shiver reflecting mine. Can a parent
mirror through unbroken change the glinting light
that rises as smoke from a chasm, wind
like ivy around the stems of a dream,
let go of wanting things a certain way, piece
together a tapestry with strands of love and grief?

Let's face it, we all await the end of grief,
when joy leaps like a humpback, apparent
as charcoal streaks against the sky. We seek peace
in objects, when we must lighten
our load, lose everything we know, let dreams
scatter as milkweed pod seeds to the wind.

The wind has stilled. Grief has vanished with the tide.
I see into darkness where peace and light wait.
Apparently I dreamt the children home.

III

Umbra

I.

A thin shell
 heaves—
a stormy sea.
Pockets of hot gas
 bubble
to the surface.

Blemishes leak black
        on a radiant face.
Grow. Split—
    fade, dissolve.

Trouble brews,
 erupts—
        now pock-marked flecks.

Opposites
packed together—
a wild shared home with
two chief spots,
        leading &
 following.

Bursting from the sun's
        radiant surface,
sun spots cool,
                darken.
Gases rise
        to the surface,
 pulled away.

Healthy, brilliant,
carried off
by the turbulence.

II.

Violent fiery blasts—
  light, radiation,
      tiny particles flung.

Motes shimmer the air in multi-
            colored curtains of light—
      greenish white tapering to pink:

Trapped—
  charged sparks
    from solar wind
            ignite
  streaks of glowing gas.
    Streamers
dance across the night sky,
  a luminous dawn.

Winter Solstice, 2000

If the doors of perception were cleansed,
Everything would appear . . . as it is, infinite.
    The Marriage of Heaven and Hell
            William Blake

Pale fingers slide on cool sands.
Bare branches shatter
in the damp lining of brittle bark.

Crows send raucous squawks
to hang in thickening dusk. We trudge
to the end of these thousand years.

Can harm and suffering live if we do not
fear them—like the cramped dark space
where Persephone waits in silence, her
terror stilled by mother's rumbled chants?

As for dark-robed Demeter, she shouts
love into the gloom, lets grain grow fertile
on once barren land. What can remain for us
but to turn our wary eyes to the shadows?

Maelstrom

Join the others.
Instant departure.
A storm cloud winging fast.

A wave of hundreds
swoops and crests. Black birds speck
on a lone pine. Half of them swirl,
turn like a wheel, flip, swish up.

>She hears the vague churn of air
>around her ears. Suspended

>does not speak, does not pray,
>breathes in the smell of ice.

Chill that flings wind, over-
throwing calm. Snow flakes cake
window screens, smear glass. Odd,
this frail sun-death.

Storm

A hawk soars above me
   shadows the grill coals that fell
      with the clay pot shards
         in the April gale.

Two mourning doves
   nestle close to a small Buddha
      head bowed
         to the earth.

There was yesterday's snow.
   The hollow shriek of the wind.
      Smashed daffodils
         against the fence.

There is my sister
   whose patch seeps morphine.
      Whose voice slows, softens.
         Becomes inaudible.

Burial

I stepped to the edge
>   the place that was bare dirt and a cloth tarp
>   the place where I could have dug my fingers in

>   as if we were sitting at the beach
>   together, letting sand tickle and fill
>   the narrow grooves between our fingers.

I sat down on the little bit of wood they'd placed
>   to keep us from falling in.

I sat on the edge of a neat grave and saw warm maple wood,
>   a Star of David, a spray of Queen Anne's lace.

I sat near her—my sister—chatted a bit the way we did.

I stepped to the edge

>   filled the void with
>   our last grains of remembered sand
>   lifted the veils of separation.

Birthday, 7.20.03

Just the sun rising on the Rockies, the
blue vastness, torn clouds—sky foam
falling out.

Do I become more of who lives inside me?

Still, a vacancy rumbles over the now.

Then birdsong. Cool breeze
settles on my fallen face.

Then the yip of a dog.

Even the grass soaks in and holds
shifts of thought, waves
rolling back forward.

Underneath, hard soil.

Lech Lecha

Genesis 11:27-12:9

What does it mean to see, to view the world
as strangers, hover over it like birds?

I study the land as it breathes with the song
and taste of salt. God will teach me to see

differently, to return to what I already
know and I will be a blessing.

Expectancy

I lift a brown blanket from my garden, find
once crackly parchment turned matted, sodden,
yellow bulb tips—fetus seedlings unfurled.

Now I cannot wait another second despite
chill alerts. How else will spring's first rays
transform them to tall stems if not right now?

My hands stumble through thick leaf clots,
birth tiny orange fingers, like that day
my baby girl dove headlong into the cool

autumn air, wrinkled, pink.
"Bring her quickly" I begged
the nurse, my heart broken open.

March Memory

When fire blazes in the sky, turns to rose ribbons,
to charcoal shreds that stain the crisp spring air,
I see my child standing

in flames. I carry her through a dark made
luminous by a house whose fire rises
with one wild surge, shoots
sparks, yellow streaks, orange flashes.

My girl lies numb and shocked on a hospital bed,
her legs turned to candle wax,
dripping skin from thigh to toe.

She grows up, she glows, she radiates light.
Her long smoldering anger flares.

Absence

Grey haze grips the hills, shears their tips,
nests in the lowlands, drifts into the lake.
Indoors, postures and breath, silence, release.

I want to ask them, the ones who knew her,
the ones who watched her sing, laugh,
cry, where she's gone.

Now mist obscures the trees.
Who holds her in the light of dawn?
Who can see through fog, vanquish clouds?

Honey Cake

Thick honey sticks
to my spoon
floats like foam
on a yellow flour sea.
I measure spoon by spoon—
the dust of leavening,
glue together
a mass of runny eggs,
gritty sugar and spice,
creating
a sweet new year cake
for my son and daughter
who do not come.

Moving Day

Today the movers vacate the last of his things—
a small wooden antique chest that held
his baseball cards and two tall teak bookcases
filled with adventure and fantasy stories where

he could hide. The rug is white, except
for the place where he'd spilled coffee that
last time he came home. I didn't mind at all.
Then he left and didn't come back.

The sun streams in. I think for a moment
I've finally put everything in order,
that the rest has been a haunted dream.
But a piece of paper flutters free from

beneath his bed, a poem he'd written as a boy,
his young words a sudden echo, a rung bell—
throbbing, contained—in the gathering dusk.

The Third Noble Truth

This is no small event, my friends' prayers
hovering above dozens of deep purple tulips
and grape hyacinth that rise up around me
from winter's hard brown crust.

I am alive and well: finches are squabbling
with mourning doves over black seed,
the spring sun pierces pink azalea buds
and splashes onto thick red brick.

My kids are living their lives, all grown.
I have only to heal, to walk, to eat
strawberries, to love and let go.

Yield

The trick is getting small enough to crawl
Inside each flower, close eyes and then let go.
When leaden memory holds you in its thrall
Hold on to greenness, love vertigo.

Within the mist of limpid early dawn
The wilted stems of daisies lift above
Damp matted grasses, drink from sun's flacon.
They take what's given, cling to nature's glove.

The present's big enough to hold a past
Of lost rooms, last yellow fields.
Light crests like waves, warms the brash
Spring buds, invents their shining yield.

What matters is that they'll open after all
Bristling with slippery shadows. That they'll fall.

Simple Gifts

Four years after his death, I open the tissue-
layered box, fitted with French painted flutes,
a wooden deer, my daughter's paper dove.

Eighteen degrees. A flicker perches on a twig,
twin hawks soar by. Brown fans,
their strong wings rise and fall.

Sun slices a path down a deserted beach, my boots
scuff. Hurricane-leveled sand hills my children
leapt from glisten, an eerie evenness now.

A friend and I prepare Cornish Hens
with rice, kale and oranges.

Notes

KAVANAH is Hebrew for intention

ANATTA is Pali for No Self

EREV ROSH HASHANAH is Hebrew for the Evening before the High Holy Day of Rosh Hashanah, the beginning of the Jewish New Year.

BARDO is a Tibetan word meaning transition or a gap between the completion of one situation and the onset of another. A period of deep uncertainty. A continuous oscillation between clarity and confusion.

DANCE: After Kun-Yang Lin's "Beyond the Bones" dance performance. Soho, New York. 6.21.03

LECH LECHA is Hebrew for Go Forth, which God said to Abram. (Genesis 12:1-17:27)

MARCH LIGHT: The line "There's just no accounting for happiness" is from the poem, "Happiness" by Jane Kenyon

THE THIRD NOBLE TRUTH: The Buddhist teaching that suffering can be overcome and happiness attained.

Acknowledgements

Martha's Vineyard Gazette: "March Light"
                                    "Erev Rosh Hashanah"
                                    "Winter Solstice"

Insight: "Stigmata"
                                    "Anatta"
                                    "Sanctuary"

Mass Audubon: "Kavanah"

"The Third Noble Truth", formally "Mother's Day", appeared in *Family Reunion, Poems about Parenting Grown Children*, Chicory Blue Press, Inc., 2003.

With profound gratitude to my readers—Laure-Anne Bosselaar, Pam Bernard, Nadia Herman-Colburn and Gary Duehr—to my teachers, and to my fellow poets who critiqued with so much care and compassion.

So many friends, students and guides have supported and believed in me, too many to mention here; but I am especially grateful to Laurie and David, and to Barbara, Deborah, Jill, Kitty, Lisa, Lucy, Narayan and Sonia for unbounded encouragement, enthusiasm and love.

Myrna Patterson was born in Cambridge, Massachusetts. After receiving her M.A. degree from Harvard University, she taught English as a Peace Corps Volunteer in Chad, Africa. She has taught for over 37 years, has written literature curriculum guides for teachers, and was a Massachusetts Cultural Council Writer-in-Residence. A Squaw Valley Community of Writers poet, Ms. Patterson has also studied with Stephen Dobyns at Vermont Studio Center, and with Marie Howe and Cleopatra Mathis at the Fine Arts Work Center in Provincetown, MA. She conducts private creative writing and poetry workshops in Cambridge and on Martha's Vineyard, and teaches at the Cambridge Center for Adult Education, and at Kripalu Center in Lenox, MA. Her website is www.howtowrite.org.

Summary

"Umbra" is a collection of poems that traces the cycles of life and death, loss and change, which are strangely like the eruption of sun spots—shadows within radiance, a kind of murkiness within all parts of life. With honesty, thoughtfulness and precision of observation, Myrna Patterson connects ordinary experience and the concrete with the natural world and the sacred. She creates a paean to the human spirit which can forgive and find acceptance, even in its bleakest moments. Writing without self-pity or blame, she says, "I sit in dark. I sit in light." Yet, "By being simple, present . . ." in this moment, transcendence is possible. Across a tapestry of fear and uncertainty, ritual and faith prevail. Ms. Patterson condenses strong feeling into compact images, demonstrating that there is great goodness, despite suffering. Love, kindness and beauty are antidotes to pain; joy can be found in nature, in dance, in flowers, in remembrance, and within the simple gifts and rhythms of everyday life.